maria

My Greatest Treasure

Rosalie
Best wishes,

My Greatest Treasure

By

Maria Louise Gaiewski

Maria Louise Gaiewski

DORRANCE PUBLISHING CO., INC.
PITTSBURGH, PENNSYLVANIA 15222

ISBN # 0-8059-6903-9
Printed in the United States of America

First Printing

For information or to order additional books, please write:
Dorrance Publishing Co., Inc.
701 Smithfield St.
Third Floor
Pittsburgh, PA 15222
U.S.A.
1-800-788-7654
Or visit our web site and
on-line bookstore at www.dorrancepublishing.com

Dedication

For
my loving family,
devoted friends,
and
my Thursday ladies.

Dedicated to
Irene Johanson.

Special thanks to
Rita Lyons.

Contents

THE NURSING HOME

Reflection

Hello, do you know me?
I was young once.
Vibrant, happy, healthy, unstoppable,
There was nothing I couldn't or wouldn't do.
I lived the American dream.
Where did it go?
What happened to my family and friends,
Children, my dear sweet children, all gone.
Am I forgotten?
Is there anyone who cares?
Sit with me,
Talk to me,
Hold my hand,
Touch my cheek.
Kiss my forehead,
Hug me,
Don't be afraid because I'm old.
I'm so lonely,
Please, please stay.
Oh my, its just a reflection.

In My Mind

Trapped in my mind
I call for help
I think
Young thoughts
Dream of first loves
Remember lost loves
Cherish memories of children
The days forever
The nights too long
I wake
To do it all again
In my mind
I am whole
In my mind
I am crying
In my mind
I am waiting
For the Angels
To take
Me
Home

Wheelchair

Long silent passageways
Always the same
Day becomes night
Night becomes day
Young grow old
Trees shed their leaves
Flowers so vibrant fade and fall
Mountains reduce to dust
Sitting on my padded perch
Watching through iron bars
I'm cared for
Hooked up
Tied up
My cage is broken
Waiting
Waiting
Waiting
They walk by
I'm not here
They don't see me
I'm not here
Soon they'll know
I can fly

My Bed of Clouds

Floating on
Pillows of clouds
Morning dew
From fallen rose petals
Kiss my lips
A distant roar of thunder
Disturbs my tranquility
Someone
Is calling my name
I'm falling
Falling into a sea of white
Still
I hear my name
Sobs
Of distant thunder
Renew my heart
Tears of joy
Touch my face
Just *for a* moment
I was free

Friend

Dear Friend,
Why are you leaving?
This time I can't come with you.
We were children together,
Running through green fields,
Tickling our toes among the tall grass.
Tumbling down sand dunes,
splashing in the ocean.
I can't remember a time we weren't together,
Dancing through life.
Grew up.
Grew old.
Soon you will leave,
I'll be so sad.
You will always be part of my heart.
Go if you must,
I know you'll be waiting for me when I come.
Your loving friend.

I Ask Myself

Is this the day?
Is everything in order?
Have I done everything?
Have I made my peace?
Have I made peace with God?
Have I forgiven?
Have I told those how much they've meant to me?
Was I the best I could be?
Have I left words of wisdom, contributions, memories?
Will I be remembered?
Have I told you how much I love you?
Have I said my good-byes?
I ask myself,
Is this the day?

The Void

Reduced to a shell
Not here
Nor there
Don't remember much
If anything
Not sure of my name
Can't remember how to dress
Walk
Eat
Talk
What shoe goes where
Every need
Tended to
There's a void
When trying to glimpse the past
Who are these people
That come and go
They cry
They smile
They whisper in my ear
They hold my hand
Such sadness
Is it today
Tomorrow
Or was it yesterday

Journey

Leaving on a journey
Long time coming
Not sure
Of date
Or time
All's made ready
Friends will come
Say their good-byes
Family remains
At my side
Waiting
This journey
I will take
Alone
I will leave
With dignity
Final destination
HEAVEN

The Couple

How can this be
I'm an elderly gentleman
Of ninety-three
There's a sweet
little lady
Lives down the hall
Always dressed fancy
Wears diamonds and pearls
Lipstick and rouge
Tells me
I'm the handsomest
Of anyone here
Not sure her eyesight
Is up to par
Wants to go dancing
Play bingo and cards
Dinner together
Every night of the week
Now
We're a couple
For all to see
HOLY MOLY
Now
She wants to
MARRY ME

WAR

War Hero

I'm drawn back
To this place
Of peace and solitude
Nothing ever changes
It remains the same
It was only yesterday
You kissed my tears goodbye
They said
It's only for a short time
You went missing
No remains could he found
Years of heartache and wonder
Such a waste
In your honor
A white granite cross
Etched with your name
Row upon row
All the same
Names fade
Memories fade
I will not come
To this place again
I still cry
Tears of a young woman
You'll always be remembered
A WAR HERO

And I Pray

A fine young soldier
Tall and handsome
Uniform of blue and gold
Rifle in hand
Sworn to serve and protect his country
Marches off to war
And I pray
A battlefield filled with carnage
Bullets, bombs, and blood
Bodies of young soldiers
Smoke, fire, and confusion
Cries for help
Silent screams
Destruction
And I pray
Fine young soldiers
Coming home to stay
All in a line
All in uniforms
All in
Flag-draped coffins
And I pray
I hear your cries
I rush to you
Hold you tight
And I pray
Please God
Not my son
He's just a little boy

My Buddy

I'm a resident
In a veteran's home
Lonely old man
Living out the day
Demons of war
haunt my dreams
Faded photographs
Memories of the past
Two young soldiers
Shoulder to shoulder
Best buddies
Another time
Another place
Served with honor
Fought with valor
My thoughts find you
Forever in my heart
I still see you
My buddy
l left you there
On the beach
At Normandy
You were barely
Nineteen

Missing in Action

l saw you
Last night
Again
In my dream
Dancing with me
At the
Village Green
Greatest love
I have ever known
Marched off to battle
Prayed every day
For your
Safe return
Prayed every day
They'd find
Your remains
Promised myself
I'd always remember
The courageous
Young Marine
Missing
Forty years
September

Split Second

A beautiful son
Born this day
Nurtured with love
Taught to be understanding
Kind
Caring
Honest
Excelled in school
Sports champion
Pillar in the community
Wonderful family man
Proud
Handsome
A mother's dream
In a
SPLIT SECOND
Gone
WAR
The telegram came today
How will I tell his
MOM

Wilma

They bombed our town
The Americans
We wanted
No part
Of the war
In Europe
Families tried to get by
They bombed continually
Nine days
Nine nights
We went underground
Hiding in shelters
Deafening sounds
Fire
Smoke
Destruction
Smells of the dying
Rationed food
Little water
Finally
The war ended
Time to rebuild
Shattered lives
Haven't seen
Haven't heard
Where was my husband?
Missing
Captured
Dead
Five long years
One day
He was standing
At my door
Erdmar Zielke 1922-1985

When

When will the headlines read:

WORLD BECOMES ONE NATION
PEOPLE BECOME ONE RACE
NOT A SINGLE SHOT FIRED
NO REPORTS OF WAR
NO ONE DIED THIS DAY
ALL IN BONDAGE SET FREE
ALL EMPLOYED
ALL CHILDREN EDUCATED
CLEAN WATER PLENTIFUL
FOOD IN ABUNDANCE
ALL ILLNESS AND DISEASE ERADICATED
PEACE ON EARTH

Now I lay me down to sleep
I pray for
Everlasting peace
And
That all is safe
In the world
Tonight

Why

Why must you
Carry that gun
Sack on your back
Full of explosives
Clothed in black
Only eyes glaring
Why must you
Point that gun
Why such hatred
Fills your heart
I know nothing
Of your war
Your beliefs on religion
Your strife
Why can't we
Live in peace
Why can't we
Love our fellow man
I'm a child
Six years old
Starting school
I will learn
WHY

Numbers

Today you became
A number
Today you became
A casualty
Today you became
A statistic
Today you became
A hero
How many monuments
Embellish the landscape
How many names
Carved on granite
How many crosses
Upon the earth
How many hearts
Broken
How many tears
Shed
How many families
Torn apart
How many names
Will they read
This day
WAR
Is not
The answer

A Letter from Daddy

1943
dear children,
your daddy misses you very much and
hopes that soon he will be home to stay.
then he can love you and play with you.
i hope you're being a good girl, baby sister too.
hope you're being a good boy.
daddy will buy you nice presents.
daddy will be home sunday morning,
wait for me,
and help mommy.
love daddy

written by my dad
Edward Yarusso

Playing

Rainy day
Two little boys
Playing upstairs
Laughing and giggling
Jumping through air
Rolling and tumbling
Making a mess
Running up and down
Cowboys and Indians
Cops and Robbers
Found
Daddy's handgun
Under the bed
One little boy
Now lays dead

Shattered

Sunny day
School is out
Two little girls
Walking on home
Bright and talented
Pretty as a picture
Ribbons and bows
Bubble gum and books
Giggling over boys
Nanny and Poppy's angel
Future of their generation
Speeding car
One shot fired
An entire family
Shattered

FRIENDSHIP AND LOVE

My Greatest Treasure

My greatest treasure
Your loyal friendship
Never to fail
In crisis or need
To give without hesitation
Bonded by a special love
Knowing each other's heart
Sharing thoughts
Sharing dreams
Laugh in good times
Together in times of peril
My greatest gift
My treasure
My dearest friend

This Place

Sandy blanket
Tousled hair
Soft sea breeze
Made love
On the beach
Counting stars
That dot
Midnight skies
Moon beams
Cast ripples
Upon the water
Swans glide by
Settling down
Among tall slender grass
Deer so gentle
Walk slowly by
Seabirds fly
Effortlessly overhead
Such undisturbed beauty
So peaceful so serene
The memory of
This place
Is tucked safely away
We shared
This place
Only
With heaven

The Moment

When was the moment
You knew
You loved me
Was it my face
My smile
That melted
Your heart
Something in my eyes
No one else saw
Can I be sure
You are the one
Maybe I'll know
How much
I love you
If I could just
Kiss you
After all
We only
Just met

Together

Dancing at the honky-tonk
Eating fried chicken
Junk food and ice cream
Fishing off the dock
Boat rides in the rain
Afternoon naps
Hugs and kisses
Making love
Swimming in the ocean
Hiking in the mountains
Vacation by the shore
Antiquing on Sunday
Flea market finds
Building a dream house
Planting trees and flowers
Fleet of old cars
Shopping for glad rags
Traipsing through the city
Movies
Plays
Picnics
Folks
Kids
Grandkids
All that exists
Is ours
Together forever
I can't imagine
Life
Without you

Wasteful Sorrow

How long has it been
This riff we're in
Can't live
Up to your
Expectations
You can't live
Up to mine
Too much alike
Too proud
To give in
Too defensible
To try
So many days
Of wasteful sorrow
Please
Now is the time
Help me to
Forgive

Thank You for Yesterday

There you were
Waiting for me
We met
Only by chance
How wonderful
To have found you
After years
Of loneliness
My heart sings
When I'm with you
Love is new again
Such devotion
Sweet tenderness
Laughing at silliness
Smiling at life
You've filled
My entire being
With hope
Today will be special
I'll spend my time
Dreaming of you
Making wishes
Planning our future
Soon we'll be together
Forever
Hugging and kissing
Today will become
Tomorrow
Thank you for yesterday

First Time

The first time
You saw me
You said
You loved me
The first time
I saw you
I knew
I loved you, too
You asked me
To dance
Held me close
Kissed my lips
You gave me
A daffodil
Every spring
When daffodils bloom
It's the first time

Never Stop

Never stop dreaming
You can change the world
Never stop thinking
You can discover a cure
Never stop learning
You can teach the masses
Never stop loving
You can procreate life
Never stop singing
You can bring joy
Never stop laughing
You can brighten the day
Never stop trying
You can do anything
Never stop praying
You can create a miracle
Never stop hoping
For peace
Never stop dreaming

Dear

Your first time
Don't be nervous, dear
It will be fine
Remove all garments
From waist up
Robe open in front
I'll return
Hello, dear
Step over here
Come in closer
Chin up
Arm over your head
Compression and pressure
Take a deep breath
Hold
Now breathe
Just two more angles
Now the right breast
Okay, dear
That wasn't so bad
You can get dressed
Doctor will be in soon
Have a seat
Hello, dear
Everything is perfectly normal
Make an appointment
One year
For a mammogram
Remember
Self-examine
It can save your life

Fine

Fine Lady
Handsome Gent
Married for life
The Angels came
Took
Fine Lady
Away
Old Gent
Sat to reminisce
Years together
Fine
Family
Home
Garden
Dog
Old Gent
Tried to
Recall
Fine Lady's name
HELL
I always
Called
Her
MOTHER

Quiet Times

I want to go back
To quiet times
Dads went to work
Moms stayed home
Played games in the street
With neighborhood kids
Climbed trees
Built forts
Rode our bikes
Walked for miles
Through the woods
Never locked doors
Knew everyone in town
School was
Kindergarten through twelve
Shopped at local
Dry good and grocery stores
Saturday matinee at the movies
Gifts were for Christmas and birthdays
Clothes where passed down
Sneakers were for gym
Sports were played at school
Ate dinner as a family
Sundays
Were for church
Dinner at Grandma's
And rest
One doctor took care of all
STUFF HAPPENED
I can't see the floor
In my
Grandchildren's bedroom

Then and Now

Years go by
You and me
Me and you
In my life
Out of my life
Never to stay
Soon you'll know
I'm the one
I told you
How much
I care
I love you
I loved you then
I love you now
I will always
Love you

Young Boy

Just a young boy
Out on his own
Hoping to find his dream
Traveled far and wide
Explored the land
Sailed the sea
Years of travel
Years of toil
Nothing satisfied his fancy
Came back
Every dream
He ever wanted
Was waiting
For him
At home

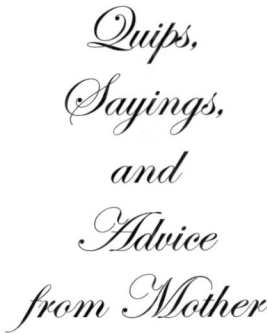

Quips,
Sayings,
and
Advice
from Mother

Don't forget to say your prayers.

There is only one person you can count on, yourself.

May the happiest days in your past be the saddest days in your
future.

Who better than you!

Do for yourself. No one is going to do it for you.

Old age does cruel things to us.

They keep us alive with technology, then they don't know what
to do with us.

Remember your manners.

Never trust a car's turn signal. Half the time the jerk behind the
wheel doesn't know it's
on.

Always go to the bathroom before you leave the house.
If you need to use the public restroom, don't touch anything.
Never sit on the toilet, and for goodness sake, wash your hands.

When the politicians get done, there won't be anything left for
the meek to inherit.

You're number one. Take care of yourself put some money away, you never know when you'll need it.

I'm sick and tired of being sick and tired.

Listen to your mother she gives the best advice.

It's not how much money you spend, it's how much money you can save.

You can't put an old head on young shoulders.

Once an adult, twice a child.

You'll appreciate your parents more when you have children of your own.

You're going to hit some potholes in the road of life.

God is so good to us. When we get old our eyesight dims, so we can't see what we look like.

Being old is bad enough, being old and poor is a tragedy.

If you can't say anything nice about a person don't say anything at all.

There are three sides to every story, her side, his side, and the truth.

You can trust a thief but you can't trust a liar.

Where there's a will there's a way.

Children can make you laugh and they can make you cry.

Don't let yourself down do your best.

We all get our turn in the barrel.

Always remember to be kind, caring and thoughtful.

Things can never be the way they used to be, they should only be better.

When you walk a mile in my shoes then you can criticize me.

Stop complaining, there is always someone with more problems than you.

Grandchildren, our reward.

Keep in touch with family, friends, and loved ones. Soon enough you'll be old.

I've become my mother.

Don't sweat the small stuff.

It only takes a moment to change your life.

Don't stay angry, life is too short.

We live in the greatest country in the world. Keep it that way —
VOTE.

If you keep things long enough they will be back in style.

Who's going to care one hundred years from now?

Take each day as it comes. Every day is a plus.

The worst thing about getting old is remembering being young.

If I knew then what I know now!

The rules are the rule. Abide by them.

You have to suffer a little to he beautiful.

I know what it feels like to be thirty, you don't know what it feels
like to be seventy.

I'm working to pay the utility bill.

Growing old ain't for sissies.

Don't believe everything you hear.

Life is a beautiful thing.

You're going to kiss a few frogs before you kiss a real prince.

Yeah, Ma, I know.

Don't make a mountain out of a mole hill.

Make every day count.

I miss you already.

My Thursday Ladies

Year after year
They still come
My Thursday ladies
For weekly coiffures
Cut and curl it
Color or perm it
Never to miss
Appointments are standing
A family like no other
Thursday is their day
Solving world problems
Discussing every imaginable subject
Laughing together
Crying and coping with sadness
Sharing hopes and dreams
Happiness is
My Thursday ladies
They tell me
They love me
I make them
Look and feel beautiful
Thank you; ladies
I love you all

A Birthday Wish from My Friend

Dear Maria,

I believe God gave you a mission, and you've been carrying it out for more years than I've been privileged to know you. A visit to your home is the therapy most of us need, and find in the time we are there, in the cheerful, caring atmosphere. We enter through Eden where we glimpse such a variety of color in the faces of flowers and arrangements, against white picket fences where we drop many cares, as we pass through your doors. I'll admit that at times I almost take it all for granted, but with this writing, all things are in focus and very clear, and I know I've been blessed. That goes for all of us who come at different hours. The animals you have cared for over the years have all been part of the experience, and they have known and know it, of course. I'm writing with the thoughts of wishing you a wonderful Happy Birthday, Maria, with blessings "aplenty" knowing how much you contribute to friends, those with four legs as well as those with two.

Love, Irene

Wild Creature

Take away the land
Chop down the forest
Pollute the water
Move them out
Make the land
Your own
Hunt them to extinction
Shoot them for trophies
Trap them for experiments
Poison them
They've become a nuisance
Wear their skins for pleasure
Put them behind bars
Watching us
Watch them
With saddened eyes
They never knew
Once upon a time
They were free
Who will speak
For the wild creatures
When their habitat is gone
Whose place is this
Last living wild creature
Known on Earth
Died this day
Born and raised
In captivity

The Mirror

She saw him
Her true love
In the mirror
A new love
Captured his heart
With tears
On her face
She watched him
Holding her close
The way he held her
Smiling in her eyes
She knew him so well
He never saw her reflection
In the mirror
Another dance
Another kiss
Why here
This was their place
Another drink
To watch her heartache
In the mirror

My House

Everyone loves coming
To my house
Cozy and charming
Protected by Angels
Happy and friendly
Loving and warm
Shaded by oaks and pines
A white picket fence
Adorned with pretty flowers
A cobblestone walk
Leads to my front door
Two amicable pooches
Wagging tails and cold noses
Are the official greeters
Come in
Make yourself at home
Kick off your shoes
Stay awhile
Pleasant conversation
Good eats
A glass of wine
Tea and cookies
Cake and coffee
Candy for the kids
Anything for you
All's welcome
At my house

Chain and Cross

I was so young
I didn't know what to do
I took you to a safe house
Someone would give you a better life
No one ever knew
I had no means to support you
Draping my chain and cross
Over your head
I kissed you good-bye
Whispering to you
How much
I loved you
I placed the basket inside the door
Then fled
Years flew by
I saw you in every child
Hoping that someday you would understand
That you would forgive me
My heart was always filled with pain
Something in the newspaper caught my eye
A familiar face smiling back at me
My face
Under the picture the caption read
"Baby Found at Safe House
On Christmas Eve
Elected State Senator"
I knew it was you
You still wore the chain and cross
I draped over your head

Mother-in-Law

I've pondered over this for years
What to call my Mother-in-Law
She's not my mother
So "Mother" is out
Won't call her "mom"
She's my husband's mom
I have my own
First name like a friend
Don't think so
Missus would be so rude
Excuse me
When needing her attention
Hey you
Won't go there
Then one day
It came to me
What a blessing
Now I call her
Grandma

Homeless

Can't seem to make ends meet
Working two jobs
Sometimes three
Wife works when she can
Never enough money
Three precious little girls
To care for
Lived in a basement apartment
Couldn't pay the rent
Kids always sick
Need money for food and medicine
Old car barely running
Looking for a decent job
An affordable place to live
Kids don't understand
Want to go back home
Lost everything when the market fell
Wife never smiles
Tries to stay strong
Such a sorry state
In a country so grand
What will become of this family
On our way to sleep
In a
Homeless shelter

Two Rotten Kids

Brothers growing up
In the same house
Different in every way
It was war
Never a day of peace
Fought all of the time
Mom and Dad
At wit's end
One was bad
The other worse
Brats through and through
Fight after fight
Didn't matter over what
They agreed to disagree
Nothing ever pleased them
The brothers grew up
They never realized
What they put
Their parents through
Until they had children
If you ask
Why they fought
Neither had a clue

Live Life

High above the rain clouds
The sun is always shining
Rain showers will cease
Cleansing our souls
Warmth from the sun
Brings us hope
And
Renews our spirit
Throw the smoldering embers
Of your life
To the wind
Scatter your daydreams
Amongst the stars
Give as much love
As you can give
Live life to the fullest
We're only here for
A very short time
The world is ours
Make every day count

Jenny

She knew she was different
People stared at her
Some turned away
Even laughing at her facial deformities
A little girl unbelievably strong
Wonderful supportive family
Numerous friends at school
Smart beyond her years
Witty and funny
A typical little girl
Years of reconstructive surgery
Years of pain and illness
Never darkened her spirit
While shopping with her mom
She saw a dress with ruffles and lace
The most beautiful dress she'd ever seen
Mom told her it was just too expensive
She made promises
Never to fight with her brother again
To keep her room spotless
If she could just have that dress
Promised she'd never ask for another thing
Another surgery
Another long hospital stay
When she returned home
A surprise awaited her
The beautiful dress with ruffles and lace
Said she'd wait for a special occasion
To show off her beautiful dress
She knew she was special
An Angel told her so
She had the dress on
When the Angel
Took her by the hand

In Loving Memory
Jennifer Walker
Age 11

Remote Control

Nothing is simple any more
What's the story
Doesn't anything go on and off
You now need a remote control
Never in my days
Were things so confusing
After forty years
Bought a new television
They even come in color
With remote control
Said to look at the menu
The last time
I looked at a menu
It had steak and ribs
The menu will teach you
Everything you need to know
To program your new T.V.
Tried and tried again
Just couldn't do it
Not my generation
To have so many gadgets
Called my eleven-year-old grandson
To come fix the mess
I made of my new T.V.